1 **Look and check.**

This animal is a

- [ ] lion
- [ ] frog
- [ ] giraffe
- [ ] bird

VOCABULARY

1 **Learn new words.** Listen and repeat. TR:01

endangered animal **species**

2 **Answer the question.** Work with a partner.

Imagine you're an animal photographer.

What endangered animals do you take pictures of?

a habitat

3 **Read and circle.**

Joel Sartore is a National Geographic **photographer / photograph**. Joel wants to help animals. How does he do that? He takes **pictures / photographer** of **habitat / endangered** animals. Joel takes photographs of many different animal **endangered / species**. Many of these animals live in zoos. They don't live in their natural **habitat / photograph**. That's why Joel can take **photographs/endangered** of them.

to take photographs / pictures

a photographer

4 **Answer the questions.**
Work with a partner.

1 What do photographers take pictures of? Name three things.

2 What do you like to take photographs of?

3 Have you ever been to a zoo? Where was it? What did you see?

NEW LANGUAGE

1 **Listen and say.** Practice with a partner. TR:02

A: Wow! That's a cool camera! **Do you like to** take photographs?

B: Yes, **I do. I like to** take photographs of my dog. Look at this!

A: That's cool! **I don't like to** take pictures. **I like to** draw.

B: What **do you like to** draw?

A: **I like to** draw bugs.

B: Bugs! Really? That's interesting!

A: Yes, it is. Bugs are amazing. Look at my drawing!

B: Wow, that's really nice!

2 **Underline.** Write true sentences.

1 I **like** / **don't like** _____ photographs of animals. (take)

2 I **like** / **don't like** _____ trees. (climb)

3 I **like** / **don't like** _____ books about animals. (read)

4 I **like** / **don't like** _____ horses. (ride)

5 I **like** / **don't like** _____ .

3 **Play a game.** Add words. Work with a group.

A: I like to take pictures.

B: I like to take pictures and play basketball.

C: I like to take pictures, play basketball, and ride my bike.

4 **Ask your classmates.**
Write their names. Talk!

> Do you like to ride a bike?

> Yes, I do.

Name	Activity	yes/no
_____	ride a bike	_____
_____	play hide and seek	_____
_____	play video games	_____
_____	take photographs	_____
_____	sing songs	_____

5 **Play Tic-Tac-Toe.** Work with a partner.

> I'm X. Juice. I like to drink juice.

> Good. Draw an X. My turn. I'm O.

5

BEFORE YOU WATCH

1 **Talk about it.** Work in pairs.

    1 Name one species of animal where you live.

    2 Name one endangered animal.

    3 Name one animal habitat.

2 Predict.

In this video, Joel Sartore talks about endangered animals. What endangered animals do you think he talks about? Work in small groups.

WHILE YOU WATCH

3 Check the names of four endangered animals you hear.

- ☐ elephants
- ☐ tarsiers
- ☐ whales
- ☐ frogs
- ☐ turtles
- ☐ tigers
- ☐ monkeys
- ☐ bugs

AFTER YOU WATCH

4 Answer the questions.

1 Name two places where Joel takes photographs of animals.

_____

2 Why are many animals endangered?

_____

3 What is the name of Joel's project?

_____

4 Why does Joel take pictures of endangered animals?

_____

5 Make a statement about the video. Say *True* or *False.* Work with a partner.

> Joel Sartore draws pictures of animals.

> False. He takes photographs of animals.

6 Answer the questions. Work with a partner.

1 Is it easier to take pictures of animals inside or outside? Why?

2 What are the difficult parts of an animal photographer's job?

3 Would you like to be an animal photographer? Why or why not?

READING

1 **Learn new words.** Listen and repeat. TR:03

rain forest   disappear   insects

2 **Look at the pictures.** What do you think the reading is about? Work with a partner.

3 **While you read**, pay attention to the animal species that in rain forest habitats. TR: 04

Endangered Habitats

A habitat is a place where animals and plants live. There are many types of habitats. A **rain forest** is one type of habitat.

Tarsiers and orangutans live in the rain forest. The rain forest is their habitat. Orangutans eat the fruit and leaves of rain-forest trees. They also eat **insects** and small animals that live in the trees. Tarsiers sleep in plants at the bottom of trees.

Rain forests and other important habitats around the world are endangered. Sometimes, people destroy a habitat because they want to use it for something else. When their habitats **disappear**, animals such as tarsiers and orangutans have nowhere to live. They can't find food to eat. In time, some of those animal and plant species may also become endangered.

a rain forest

AFTER YOU READ

4 **Answer the questions.**

1 Which animal needs tall trees to sleep in?

_____

2 What can hurt or destroy a habitat?

_____

3 What happens to the plants and animals in a habitat that has been destroyed?

_____

4 Where do tarsiers sleep?

_____

5 Why are orangutans and tarsiers endangered?

_____

5 **Talk it over.** What did you learn about habitats? Work with a partner.

> People can destroy habitats.

6 **Answer the questions.** Work in a small group.

1 What habitat does your favorite animal live in? Is that habitat disappearing? Is the animal endangered? Explain.

2 People live in habitats, too. What kind of habitat do you live in? Do you live in a city or town, or in the country? Describe your habitat.

9

Photo Ark

"I want people to care, to fall in love, and to take action."

1 **Learn new words**. Listen and repeat. TR:06

unusual   portrait   beautiful

2 **Listen and read.** TR:07

Animal Portraits

Joel Sartore takes **unusual** photographs of animals for The Photo Ark. These special pictures are called **portraits**. A portrait is a picture that shows the face of a person or animal.

When you look at a Photo Ark portrait of an animal, you see the animal's eyes. Joel wants people to look into the eyes of the animals. He wants people to see that all animals are **beautiful**. He wants people to care about them.

3 **Answer the questions.** Work with a partner.

Do you think photographs can help endangered animals? Why or why not?

4 **Complete the sentences.** Work with a partner.

1 I like to look at _____ of famous people.

2 Kangaroos have a very _____ way of walking.

3 I think flowers are _____.

5 **Check the things you care about.** Ask and answer.
Work with a partner.

☐ sea animals

☐ endangered animals

☐ my pet

☐ my family

☐ my school

☐ _____

> I care about recycling. How about you?

> I care about clean water.

6 **Ask and answer.** Work in small groups.

1 How can people help endangered animals? Say two things.

2 Where you live, what do people do to help animals? Say one thing.

3 What do you want people to care about? Why?

> What do you care about? Do you care about endangered elephants?

> I care about endangered gorillas and elephants!

Choose an activity.

A Take a photograph of an animal.

- Take a photograph of an animal, including bugs.
- Write a paragraph about that animal for your school's website.
- Show your photo to the class.

B Record an interview. Work with a partner.

- Choose an endangered animal at a zoo or rescue center.
- Write questions and answers for an interview.
- Role-play the interview with the person taking care of the animal. Record it.
- Play the recording for the class.

C Make a video. Work with a group.

- Choose an endangered animal.
- Write three facts about it.
- Record each member talking about their animal.
- Play the video for the class.

EXTRA

What did you learn from your classmates? Write two things.

1 _____

2 _____

Work with a partner. Play the game. Name the endangered animal or the habitat. Use a coin.

Move 1 space.   Move 2 spaces.

START

FINISH

PROJECT

1 **Make an endangered animal mobile.**

- Research three endangered animals.

- Write a sentence about each animal on a card.

- Draw or find pictures of the animals.

- Use string to attach the animal pictures and sentences.
- Hang them on your mobile.

Endangered animals

Bengal tigers
Bengal tigers live in forests in India.

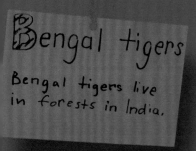

Giant pandas
Giant pandas live in bamboo forests in China.

African elephants
African elephants live in rain forests, deserts, and grasslands.

2 Present your mobile to the class.

3 Say one thing about these things. Work with a group.

☐ Joel Sartore

☐ The Photo Ark

☐ endangered animals

☐ animal habitats

☐ how I can help the animals

GLOSSARY

beautiful:
very pretty
Example: *I think insects are beautiful!*

disappear:
We can't see this anymore.
Example: *Endangered species such as the northern white rhino may soon disappear.*

endangered:
There are not many (of this animal) in the world.
Example: *A tarsier is an endangered animal.*

a habitat:
the place where a plant or animal lives
Example: *The habitat of camels is the desert.*

insect:
a very small animal that has six legs
Example: *Spiders are not insects, but ants are!*

a photographer:
someone who takes photographs
Example: *Joel Sartore is a photographer.*

portrait:
a painting, drawing, or photograph of a person or animal
Example: *You can take a portrait of a pet such as a dog or cat.*